CRUSHES

dating, rejection, and other stuff

by Nancy Holyoke
illustrated by Elisa Chavarri

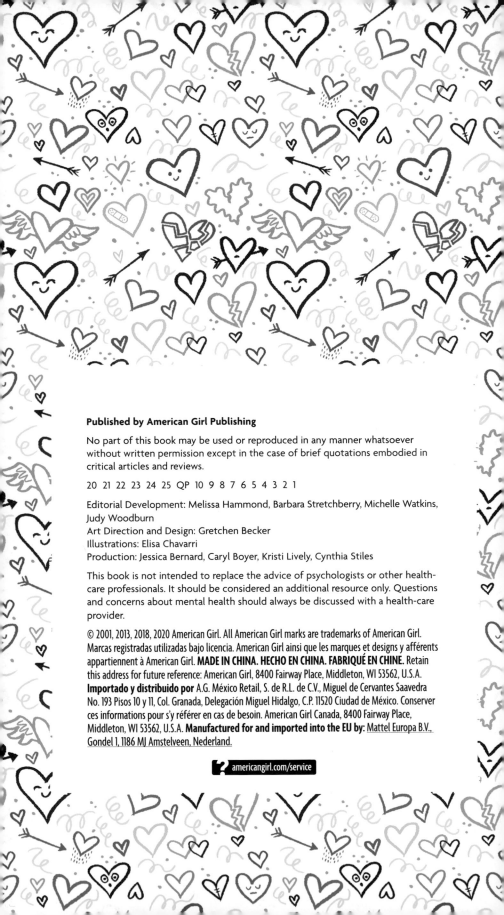

Editorial Development: Melissa Hammond, Barbara Stretchberry, Michelle Watkins, Judy Woodburn
Art Direction and Design: Gretchen Becker
Illustrations: Elisa Chavarri
Production: Jessica Bernard, Caryl Boyer, Kristi Lively, Cynthia Stiles

This book is not intended to replace the advice of psychologists or other health-care professionals. It should be considered an additional resource only. Questions and concerns about mental health should always be discussed with a health-care provider.

Dear Reader,

Romance. It was always out there. You've seen it between people. You've read about it. You've seen it on-screen. You may have even had glimmers of those feelings yourself. But mostly you've sailed along among friends and classmates, kids you know well and kids you don't, doing what kids do. Romance was for later.

Now that's changing. Kids are getting **crushes.** Your friends are talking about who likes who. Your body's changing, and so are your emotions. A kid you've known forever gives you a look, and all of a sudden you're nervous and excited—and confused.

Of course you've got **questions.** What do you say to somebody you've got a crush on? How can you tell if a person likes you? What if you have no crushes, while your best friend has five a day? What about parties? Dances? Dating? And what, oh what, about rejection?

This book is a guide for all these things. It was first published some years ago as *A Smart Girl's Guide: Boys.* This edition has some new information and a new title. But its goal is the same. You want to feel good and be yourself in this crazy new world. You want to be part of the fun without losing your pride or your brain or your heart. We hope this book will make it easier for you to do that.

Your friends at American Girl

contents

couples 81

taking care of you 105

brave
new world

crushes

Lots of kids—boys and girls alike—have crushes from the time they go off to preschool. But as you reach puberty, those crushes may get bigger. Tiny crushes, which in first grade took up a corner of your brain, can

become **huge, humongous, gigantic**

crushes that make you look out the window for hours instead of studying for your math test.

Lots of crushes are daydreams. You might have a crush on a pop star. You might have a crush on a teacher or your cousin in Omaha. You might have a crush on a kid at school who doesn't even know your name. These kinds of crushes can make you feel **wonderful** because . . .

you have **excited,** happy feelings,

you have fun **imaginings,**

you can feel romantic about someone **without the risk** that that person might hurt your feelings **(it's safe),**

and you will never have to face the fact that your crush is **not perfect.**

Crushes are also useful. A crush lets you try on new feelings, sort of like trying on clothes in a store. You can learn a lot without buying anything. You consider what you like in other people. You learn how to deal with frustration when you can't get what you want. It's all part of growing up.

Of course, you also might develop a crush on someone you actually know. Kids around you may be getting crushes, too. Some might even be speaking up and saying so. This can make life at school very different.

a typical day

Suddenly kids are talking about who likes who. School is a more gossipy, less private place. There's more intrigue—and more nervousness, too.

8:45 a.m.	Sophia tells Addison she likes Ryan.
10:05 a.m.	Addison tells Ryan that Sophia likes him. Ryan says, "Uh, well, Sophia's OK."
10:36 a.m.	Maria writes her favorite movie star's name on her notebook cover for the 348th time.
11:05 a.m.	Addison sends a text to ten of her closest friends (including Sophia) announcing that Sophia and Ryan are now together.
11:47 a.m.	Taylor sits near Destiny at lunch. That's new. What does it mean? Destiny has no idea.
11:50 a.m.	Sophia says hi to Ryan in the cafeteria. Ryan says hi back. They both sit with their friends.
12:01 p.m.	Max and Gabriella ignore each other when they dump their trays. They are neighbors and good friends, but they never let on at school because they'd be teased.

1:30—1:45 p.m.	Sophia writes a note to Ryan and folds it up till it's the size of a wad of chewing gum. She gives it to Addison to deliver.
2:10 p.m.	Kayla and Jing and Autumn have a good time in gym teasing David and DeShay and Reese.
3:00—3:30 p.m.	Addison gives Sophia's note to Ryan. She thinks he looks cute when he's embarrassed. On the bus, Addison makes a list of all the kids she's liked this year. It looks like this:

1. Ryan (2 weeks)
2. Tyler (1 week)
3. Khalid (2 days)
4. David (3½ hours)
5. Maggie's brother Jonathan (in her dreams)

There were others first semester, but she lost count. She thinks maybe she'd like to go with Ryan again after he and Sophia break up. She figures her friend and her new crush will last about **two weeks.** Maybe **one.**

hormones

What is causing all this drama? For one thing, hormones.

Hormones are chemicals in the body. During puberty, a girl's hormones help her body develop into a woman's body, and a boy's hormones help his body develop into a man's body. In general, this happens a little sooner for girls. That's why girls are sometimes taller and physically more mature than boys up until high school.

Hormones cause lots of **emotional changes,** too. Your moods get stronger at the same time your body's growing in new, confusing ways. Throw in all the other things kids are often dealing with at this age—acne, body odor, braces. Small wonder if a girl finds romantic feelings hard to handle.

After
hormones

Before
hormones

- Eye contact is normal.
- Thinking is normal.
- Talking is no big deal.

- Eye contact is iffy.
- No clue what to say.
- Heart is jumpy.
- Stomach is woozy.
- Thinking? Ha!

staying normal

I don't have any problem being myself around girls, but sometimes when boys are around, I can't seem to be me. I just act weird.

Breena

A lot of girls find it hard to act normal. The simplest thing—like passing an assignment to the kid in the next desk—may send clouds of questions rolling through your mind.

11

weird-o-meter

You start acting, **well, weird.** But there are ways you can control that.

galloping giggles

Jesse cracks a joke. You go heeheeheeheeheeheeheeheehee heeheeheeheeheeheeheeheeheeheeheeheeheeheehee heeheeheeheeheeheeheeheeheeheeheeheeheeheehee—and can't stop until the teacher walks up and raps on your desk.

A good joke deserves a good giggle. Lots of us may laugh when we're nervous, too, whether something's funny or not. That's OK up to a point, but you don't want to be the kid who giggles all the time. It makes you seem silly. And you're just not good company when you're out of control. So when the giggles attack, close your mouth, freeze your chest, and hold your breath for a moment. Glance away. Do something with your hands—grab a pencil, fool with the straps of your backpack. Concentrate on pulling yourself together, and don't let go till you do.

being fake

Nicholas is cute, Nathan is awesome, and Neo is cool. You have to walk past them all on the way to your locker. You put your chin in the air, pretend you're Miss Popularity, and hope they buy the act.

Most of us put up a front when we're nervous. It helps us hide our fears. But the goal is to relax and be yourself, not to pass yourself off as Miss Popularity. So don't overdo the cool. Release that chin. Picture yourself the way you are coming off the field after a winning game, singing along to your favorite song, or talking to your little sister. Picture you being you.

chatterbox

Angel is standing next to you in line. Suddenly you hear yourself jabbering away as if your mouth weren't connected to your brain.

Slow down. It will give you time to think before you speak. Don't run your words together. Take a breath between sentences. Ask questions. Conversations involve both people talking, after all. While Angel's responding, really listen. That will help you decide what to say next.

avoidavoidavoid

C.J. and Matt are so cute! They're talking to your best friend during a break in gym. You'd like to join them, but what if you say the wrong thing? What if they think you're butting in? You stay where you are and count bricks in the wall.

Try not to avoid boys. It will only make your nerves worse. Remind yourself that it's natural for girls and boys to feel fluttery around one another at this age. For that matter, it's natural to feel fluttery around anyone you're crushing on. The way to learn to talk to people you find attractive is to talk to them. Practice makes perfect. Or at least with a little practice, talking to a crush won't be such a big deal.

"liking" someone

I have a group of really great friends who are each unique and creative in their own way. Some of them happen to be boys. There's this one kid I've known since the third grade, but now that we're getting older, I'm starting to like him differently (if you know what I mean).
Meg

You've always had certain feelings about the people around you. You liked some a little, others a lot. That's still true, only now **romantic feelings** come and go by the day. Is that kid you have fun talking to a "friend" or something else? All of a sudden, you might not be quite sure. Answers to some basic questions would be nice.

a few basics

Q. Boys and girls are the same, but they're different, too. What gives?

A. Every person is an individual. Any boy, any girl, can be anything and do anything that's humanly possible. People are amazingly varied. When it comes to the person in front of you, there's no way to say, "He's this, she's that."

But it's also true that, as a group, boys are different from girls in certain ways. Some of those differences are physical. For instance, scientists have shown that girls' brains and boys' brains are different, physically and chemically. And boys have different hormones, which make for different emotions. Other differences are learned. From the time they're babies, boys and girls get different messages about who they should be. Those messages vary widely depending on their families, where they live, and the times they're growing up in. But what's always true is that people's surroundings help shape who they are. So are boys and girls both the same and different? Yes.

Q. Stereotypes are a problem. "Girls like to wear pink" is a stereotype. But you do like pink. What should you do?

A. If you like pink, by all means wear pink. There's nothing in the world wrong with that. What's important is that the boy in the next desk can wear pink, too, if he wants to. A kid should get to pick what he or she likes best. That goes with clothes, hair, games, foods, books—whatever. We're all unique. Kids shouldn't feel stuck with choices they don't like because that's what boys and girls are "supposed" to be or do.

Q. Do all girls like boys?

A. No. Some girls get crushes on other girls. Some get crushes on both boys and girls. Others don't get crushes at all. The same variety exists with boys. It's all normal.

Q. Do you have to announce whether you're straight or gay or whatever, like on a sign-up sheet?

A. No. The point is not to find the right label. The point is to understand what makes you happy. So just pay attention to your feelings and form the relationships that seem right for you. If the day comes when you want to embrace a word for that, you can do so then.

Q. Does everybody agree on stereotypes, the differences between girls and boys, and who can like who?

A. No. But we should all be able to agree that every person deserves respect. A lot of bad stuff happens when people look at one another and think, *They're different from me, they shouldn't be like that.* Being different isn't bad. It's what people *are*. That's why the Golden Rule remains gold. Treat others the way you want to be treated yourself.

Q. How can you get someone to like you? You're thinking you need a makeover.

A. Attraction is a bit mysterious. Looks count, but not as much as you might think. Ask a bunch of kids what they look for in another person, and you'll hear:

> a good personality

> someone attractive, nice, and with a good sense of humor

> smart, cute, fun to be around

> someone who likes me for me

> girls who are themselves—who aren't all phony and stuff

So go ahead and experiment with your looks. But before you buy a bucket of makeup or drop old friends for new ones to impress that special someone, ask yourself, "Is this going to make me happier to be me?" If the answer is no, don't do it. The most attractive things about a person have to do with character—basics such as kindness, humor, and honesty. Set your sights on that, and the rest will take care of itself.

beginnings

If you're curious about a person, **be friendly.** Run a smile up the flagpole. Say hi in the hall.

Get a **conversation** going. Do you wish your teachers would teach you more about Vikings? Say so. Is your science project melting? Crack a joke about it. Talk about the basketball game or your favorite show. Ask some questions. See where they lead.

Look for common interests, too. Do you both love sci-fi? Play the same video game? Enjoy the same music? Run track? Find out **what you share.**

Better yet, **do something** while you're talking. It's easier to feel relaxed with a person if you're playing Ping-Pong or practicing your lines for the class play—not just staring at each other trying to think of what to say.

the big fear

I really, really, really like this boy in my class, but I'm afraid to tell him that I like him. I'm afraid he'll say something like "Gross!" or tell his friends and everyone will laugh at me.
Boy Crazy in Illinois

For some girls, having a crush is a private thing. They're not ready to go public with how they feel. Other girls would like their crush to know, if they weren't afraid of one little thing.

Everybody worries about it. Nobody wants to get hurt. Nobody wants to be embarrassed. Nobody wants to find out that the person she's had a crush on doesn't feel the same way about her. It's always a gamble to let someone know how you feel. But you can cut your risk a lot if you pay attention to the signs your crush is sending before you speak up.

reading the signs

Funny looks

I really like this one guy. Just about every time he sees me, he gives me this long (not mean) stare. Is this good or bad? Sight or Fright?

Staring could be good. It could also mean your shirt tag is hanging out. Find an excuse to talk to him. Say something about the Science Olympiad or the Hawaiian Surprise pizza at lunch. See what happens. Maybe he'll grunt and turn away. Maybe he'll grin and blush and tell you what he did with the pineapple he scraped off his pizza. Either way, you'll have your answer.

Girl crush

I think I have a crush on a new friend in my art club. I want to spend more time with her, because she makes me feel good when we're together. But I don't want to embarrass either one of us by asking her out if she doesn't like girls. Club Romance

You want to spend more time with this girl, so do. Get to know her better. Sit together at lunch. Share homework time. If your family's doing something special, invite her along. Do all the things you'd do with any friend. The more time you spend together, the more time there will be to talk. Eventually, you'll know how she feels about boys, girls, crushes, and more. Whether you two end up a couple or not, you'll have a wonderful new friend.

No, no, no

I have a boy problem, and I don't know what to do. He's really cute, nice, and unbelievably sweet. Oh, and he's really funny. He doesn't like me like I like him, but he said we should be really good friends. That's OK. Just one problem. He doesn't talk to me or do anything with me, and sometimes he avoids me.

Boy Prob

When your heart's saying yes, yes, yes, it can be hard to see that a boy's trying to say no, no, no. You have to look at his actions, not just his words. This boy wants to be nice, friendly, and respectful. But he doesn't want to be your boyfriend, and by the sound of it, he doesn't want to be "really good friends" either. So save yourself some heartache and look somewhere else.

Wise guy

There's this boy that I like, and I think he likes me, but I'm not sure. For example, at recess he says, "Hi, Goofy." But he also unfreezes me when we play freeze tag with our friends. What should I think?
Not Sure About Love

Boys often express affection for their friends by kidding around. They may do the same thing with a girl they like. A boy who teases you in a fun way could indeed have a crush on you. If he says "Hi, Goofy," and makes a big point of unfreezing you at tag, chances are good.

Shy guy

My friends and I have a crush on this one boy. He's very shy and won't admit who he likes. We've asked him many times, and we've told him we like him. What should we do?
Clueless

It could be that this boy is shy. It could be that he feels about girls the way you felt about boys two years ago—indifferent. In either case, if he wanted a romantic relationship with you or your friends, he would have spoken up by now. To question him again and again is only going to embarrass him. For now, cross him off your list.

saying "I like you"

You've been watching for signs. You think your crush might like you. You're ready to say how you feel. But how? You don't want the whole world to know. A message could get passed around. Your friends might gossip if you get them involved. No, the best thing is to tell the person yourself. And here's how you can do that:

★ You and your crush are on the bus. You can say, "Isn't your football team playing tonight? Maybe I'll come watch."

★ You're both at the pool. Ask, "OK if I put my towel next to yours?"

★ The party's on, and the music's going. Go ahead and ask! "Want to dance?"

★ You and your friends are getting ice cream after school. Send a text: "You could meet us there if you like."

★ You've got an extra ticket to the concert. You can say, "Want it?"

- ★ The bell's about to ring. You can say, "A bunch of us are playing basketball after school. You should join us."

- ★ It's the school carnival. Say, "I challenge you to the rubber-duck ringtoss. Best two out of three. Loser buys pizza."

- ★ You just saw a video online of an opossum and a ketchup bottle. Send the link, adding, "This cracked me up."

- ★ Science presentations were today. You can say, "I liked your report. I didn't know dust mites were so cool. Maybe we can work on the next project together."

But where, you may ask, are the words "I like you"? Nowhere.

You don't need a big declaration to let someone know how you feel. It's going to be perfectly clear because you're being so friendly. If your crush is interested, your invitations will be accepted. If not, they won't. But it will be a whole lot easier on your feelings to hear "No, I can't go for ice cream" than "No, I don't like you."

5 mistakes

An overenthusiastic girl can turn a person off. Play it smart and avoid these classic mistakes.

1. Don't follow your crush around all the time. It's annoying. Give the kid some air.

2. The same goes with phones. Don't bury this person in messages. Don't text every hour. And don't talk forever on a call, either. A short, fun conversation is better than a long one where you're both straining to think of things to say.

3. Avoid flattery. "You're funny" is fine. But go on for ten minutes on the subject, and you're laying it on too thick.

4. "You should like me" doesn't work. You're in charge of your feelings, but you're not in charge of anyone else's. You can't pressure someone into liking you.

5. The day may come when you're tempted to snub a friend or badmouth someone in order to impress a crush. Don't. You don't like catty people or disloyal friends. Your crush won't, either.

getting no for an answer

If you get no from someone you like, **it hurts.** A lot. There's no question about it. And it can be humiliating, too—especially if you get the news in the lunchroom in front of an audience. You're going to feel like crawling away and hiding in your backpack.

Do

What you need to do, though, is:

★ Act as if it's **no big deal.**

★ Smile and say, "Oh, well. **That's OK."**

★ If you feel like crying, find a **private place** where you can do it without the world watching. But make an exception for that one special friend who can comfort you.

★ Crack a **joke.** It's a way of telling other people you're not going to collapse because of one turndown—and a way of telling yourself that, too.

★ Get **busy** with something else—schoolwork, talking to a friend, riding your bike. Diving into an activity will take your mind off your feelings and help hide your hurt.

Don't

What you don't want to do is:

★ Argue or **plead.** It won't change your crush's mind. It will only make you look needy.

★ Get **mad,** say nasty things, and treat this person like an enemy.

★ Feed a **drama.** You'll want to talk to your friends, but you don't want them running around, carrying messages, and blowing things up into an extravaganza that the school will be talking about all week.

★ Let people drag you into big **discussions** about how miserable you must feel. It will make you even more miserable.

★ **Imagine** that you'll get a different answer if you ask again next week.

saying no

There's this boy at school, and he's really weird. Nobody likes him. He makes these weird snorting noises. I always have to sit next to him. Today he asked me out. I don't want to hurt his feelings. What do I do?
Scared to Say No!

Unless you've got a heart like a turnip, turning somebody down isn't easy to do. But you don't want to get stuck in a relationship that makes you unhappy just because you didn't have the nerve to speak up for yourself. It's got to be said. So say it right.

Use your manners.
You can turn down this invitation the way you'd turn down any other. Give this person your attention and use polite words: "I'm sorry, but I'm busy after school."

Be clear and direct.
"No, I'm sorry. You're nice, but I don't want to be your girlfriend" is better than "Uh, I don't know, I don't think so, right now, you know, maybe. Sorry." You don't want to create confusion. And don't say you want to be friends unless you do.

You don't owe anyone a yes.
If a boy keeps hanging around when you wish he wouldn't, talk to him with stronger language: "I've said no, and you should accept that. You are embarrassing me and pressuring me. I don't like it. You have to stop."

Keep it private.

Don't blast the news all over school or let your friends do so, either.

Do NOT make fun of this kid with your friends.

But what if the person is really, really geeky and weird and ugly and unpopular and embarrassing, and you can't even begin to believe that he would talk to you, and you never, ever in this lifetime would have anything to do with him, and you want to be sure everybody on the planet knows that?

The answer: Be as nice and respectful as you would be to anyone else.

Every kid has feelings—feelings just like yours. It takes a lot of courage to tell someone you like them. Talking someone down for that is a rotten thing to do.

is there a rule?

Q. Is there a set age when it's OK for a girl to date?

A. No. Every family has its own ideas about this. So talk to your parents. Pick a time that's made for talking—when you're in the car, say, or folding laundry before bedtime. Tell your mom or dad a thing or two about kids crushing at school. Ask your parents about their own first crushes. Once you've broken the ice on the subject, it will be easier to ask your questions. Listen carefully to be sure you're all talking the same language. To you, "dating" may mean that two people acknowledge that they like each other. To your parents, "dating" might mean that two people go out on actual dates and spend lots of time alone together. If you're, say, 12, your parents may be OK with the first kind of relationship but not OK with the last.

Q. You really like this guy you met in your youth group. He's a couple of years older than you. Is that a problem?

A. Yes. A big one. Lots of girls get crushes on older boys. Flirting with a friend's older brother or the lifeguard at the pool is as traditional as sun in August. You both know it's a game. You're out to have fun, and that's it. And that's fine.

But is it OK to have an actual romantic relationship with an older guy? No. No way. It doesn't matter how nice he is. He's at an entirely different stage of growing up. He's far more experienced than you are. He's much stronger physically. It cannot be an equal relationship or anything close to one.

Q. When should a person come out? You're gay but afraid to say so. It's lonely, but it seems safer to be invisible.

A. You're lonely, yet you're far from alone. There are lots of kids like you up and down the halls—kids who are hiding their sexual feelings and sense of identity because they're afraid they'll be teased or bullied if they didn't. And it's true—they might be harassed. Not at every school, but at many. Not by all kids, but by some. You have to do what feels right to you, based on your own situation.

That said, staying private doesn't have to mean being isolated. Talk to an adult you trust. It could be a parent. It could be a counselor at school. Ask if he or she can help you find a safe place online where you can talk to other gay kids. There could also be local clubs you could join. Having a community where you feel safe to express yourself will be a huge relief. It will make you more confident, too. Eventually, you might decide you're ready to tell a friend or two at school, and your community of support will grow.

These strategies should get you through to high school. By then, chances are that you'll find less teasing, more acceptance, and lots more kids who feel relaxed about both who they are and who you are.

talking to parents

You want your parents to hear what you have to say. These strategies can help.

AVOID: The explosion.

I have to go. I already said I would. How can I tell them? We've talked about it all week! Everybody will hate me! You're wrecking everything!! I won't have any friends!!! I hate you!!!!

INSTEAD: Go slow.

When you're upset, it's easy to let your words take off like a runaway train. Your story gets garbled and your emotions hot. None of that is going to improve things. So slow down. Choose your words carefully. If you stay calm, you'll be more persuasive. Your parents will notice your maturity, and that will keep them listening.

AVOID: Pouncing.

You mean I can't date? All my friends can date!

INSTEAD: Listen.

You want your parents to listen to you. You have to listen to them. Give them their turn to talk. If you can talk through the details, you may find you agree on more than you thought you did.

You don't get it.

INSTEAD: Try again.

If you shut down the conversation by declaring it's hopeless, your parents may never really understand your point of view. Hang in there. Take a deep breath. Take another one. Try again. Be patient.

AVOID: Threats and accusations.

You treat me like a baby! You can't stop me!

INSTEAD: Hit pause.

There will be times when you run out of self-control and are about to say things you'll regret. So take a break. Say, "I need to cool down for a bit," and go to your room. Pound your pillow if you need to. Then get out some paper and start planning what you'll say when you come back out.

AVOID: The freeze-out.

INSTEAD: Keep talking.

Not all conversations end well. People have to come back to the issue another day. Or another week. That's OK. The important thing is that you don't hole up behind a wall of silence and stop communicating. Make a pact with your parents: No matter how much you disagree, you'll always hear each other out. There's a long future stretching ahead of you and your family. So keep in touch. You'll be glad you did.

are you crush crazy?

What sounds most like you? Circle your answer.

1. Dylan sits down at the table behind you.
- **a.** Your stomach does a flip-flop, but you keep talking with your friends.
- **b.** You say, "Ooh-ooh-ooh. There he is!" and keep talking with your friends.
- **c.** You squeal and laugh till Dylan overhears you and moves to another table. Your friends are more embarrassed than you are.

2. You're at the pool with your friends when Xavier shows up.
- **a.** You say hi when he swims past your water-basketball game.
- **b.** You watch him out of the corner of your eye. When he goes to the snack bar, you snag a friend and follow.
- **c.** Friends? What friends? You're going to stick to this guy like fresh gum. Why else would you be at the pool to begin with?

3. There's a big science test tomorrow.
- **a.** You study for it.
- **b.** You call a friend and gossip for a half hour about your crush. Then you study for the test.
- **c.** You call Mike twice, Muneeb three times, and Joel four. You glance at your science notes and then call a friend to tell her what the boys said.

4. You've always wanted to learn to paddleboard. Now the youth group's at the lake and you have your chance. Sarah is there, too.
- **a.** You head straight for the dock to learn the boarding basics.
- **b.** You spend an hour trying to talk Sarah into getting wet.
- **c.** You stay on the shore. If Sarah isn't paddleboarding, you aren't, either.

5. You text all the kids you like.
- **a.** You send two texts.
- **b.** You send four.
- **c.** You're still texting.

Answers

Self-reliant

If you answered mostly **a's,** you've got things to do, places to go, and friends to see. If a romance turns up along the way, that's great. But if not, that's OK, too. You've got an independent spirit and a healthy self-respect. Other people will like you for it. Better yet, you'll like yourself.

Wishful

If you answered mostly **b's,** you're willing to make some compromises for a crush. But spend your time running after someone? Not you.

Carried away

If you answered mostly **c's,** your head's so full of crushes that there's not much room for anything else. Surely, that's not what you want. You know that happiness doesn't come from getting the right crush to call. It comes from feeling good about what you can do and working toward things you care about. So force your eyes away from that kid at the next desk. Bend your mind back to paddleboarding and hydrogen molecules and the business of being you.

life in the fishbowl

among friends

You and this one kid have been hanging out. You aren't a couple exactly. But *something's* happening. Who will help you figure it out?

EVERYBODY.

There are your friends.

And this kid's friends.

Not to mention the rest of the school. Sit with someone new at lunch, and everybody in the state has heard about it by the time you get on the bus. It's like living in a fishbowl. You're always on view. Everyone knows what everyone else is doing—and has an opinion about it.

Your friends may think the person you like is just fine. (They may even have the exact same crush you do.) They may think you've fallen for a lower life-form (and tease you till you wonder what you've been thinking).

What they probably won't do is keep quiet. One way or another, the minute you hatch a romance, your friends are going to be involved with that relationship, too.

changing interests

My best friend is angry because I like a boy. How can I like a boy without breaking our friendship and losing someone I trust?
Worried

I've been best friends with this girl for three years. Now we're in sixth grade. But she's changed. Now that she's got a boyfriend, it's as if I'm not even there. We used to do everything together.
Left Out

You and your friend may have shared secrets and sleepovers since first grade, but if one of you is having crushes and the other isn't, there can be days when you feel like strangers. All of a sudden, the two of you are looking at each other and wondering where the magic went.

rx for an ailing friendship

If you're crushing and your friend isn't:

★ Don't ask a crush to come along every time you go somewhere with your friend. **Save time** just for her.

★ Don't text nonstop with a crush when you're with your friend. Pull away from your phone and **pay attention** to her.

★ Don't talk about your crushes **constantly.** At best, you'll be boring. It may also make your friend feel jealous and left out.

★ Don't **break a date** with your friend because a crush asks you to do something else. It's hurtful and rude.

★ Don't tell your friend that everything would be fine **if she liked somebody,** too. She shouldn't have to do something she feels uneasy about just to please you.

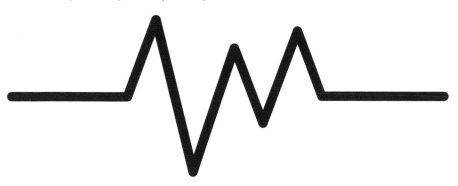

If you aren't having crushes but your friend is:

★ It's easy to get jealous. Remind yourself that friends and crushes are **different** types of relationships. The fact that your friend is having romantic feelings shouldn't make her like you any less.

★ Be **patient.** Some girls go crush crazy for a while and then calm down. Give it time.

★ Try **sharing.** If you can accept the fact that your friend wants to spend time with new people, and be cheerful when they turn up, you may find yourself having a good time, too.

popularity

Of course, it isn't just your friends you need to live with. There are all those other kids out there—especially the popular kids. It's like the whole school is tuned to the **Popularity Channel** all day, all the time.

If you're "popular," it feels pretty good (although not as good as other kids may imagine it does). If you aren't "popular," you probably have mixed feelings about the kids who are.

Obsessing about popularity can warp a girl's sense of herself. It can also give her **warped ideas** about dating. For example:

"Dating makes you more popular."

Not true! *The popular girls date, so if I date, I'll be popular.* That's the logic, but it's faulty. Having an official Someone isn't going to make you any more popular than would getting new boots. You can't accessorize your way to popularity. You plus one is still going to be you, only you'll be tangled up in an insincere relationship, and that never feels good.

"If you start dating, it had better be a kid who's at least as popular as you are. Otherwise, your own popularity will go down."

Not true! The only kind of popularity that's worth anything comes from respect. The best way to gain the respect of other kids is to act with independence and confidence. A good way to lose it is to weigh people's popularity before you decide who you want to hang out with.

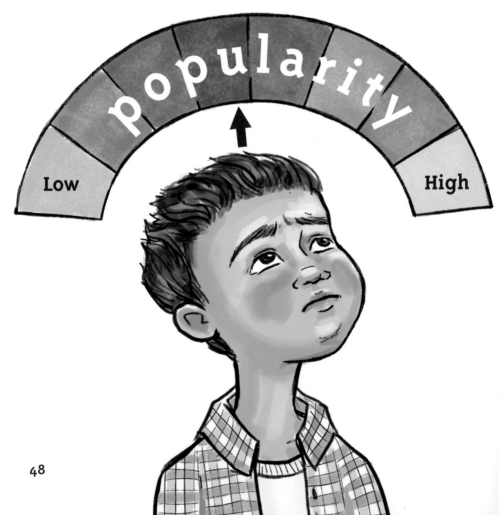

"The best kids to date are the popular kids."

Not true! Great kids come in all kinds of flavors—kind, funny, considerate, smart, sweet, interesting, brave, talented, amazing . . . But "popular" isn't one of them.

Funny

Smart

Brave

Considerate

Sweet

Lots of wonderful kids are popular. But a jerk can be popular, too. And a jerk is a jerk.

HELLO my name is

Jerk

boy buds

There's a boy at school, and we're like best friends. I tried to say this to another friend. She said, "That's what they all say." Now people at school are suggesting this boy and I go out. I wouldn't mind, except I don't want to ruin a great friendship.

Torn

A year ago, being friends with a boy was no big deal. Now everyone wants to make something of it. "Is he your boyfriend?" "Are you two together?" Some kids just won't leave you alone.

Point Number 1

Having a guy friend is a great thing. It gives you a chance to relax and get to know a boy without the feelings and responsibilities that come with a romance. It means you'll have fewer misconceptions about boys if you decide to date one. You don't want to throw all that away just because some people find it entertaining to make you uncomfortable.

No, we're just friends.

So don't. You know what you're doing. Look the teasers in the eye and say, "No, he and I are just friends." Do the same thing the next 85 times these people ask the question. Eventually, they'll get bored and move on.

Point Number 2

It's also true that if people around you are pairing up, you may look at your (boy) friend and think, *Well, I do like him, so maybe.*

Pairing up with a friend sometimes works out great. Friendship is the foundation of all good relationships. You two already know something about each other's likes and dislikes. You know how to have fun together. That's all helpful. At the same time, being a couple can be a lot more complicated than being friends.

Other people may try to tell you what to do.

And what you expect from each other may change.

Sometimes two kids will start dating and find that they had more fun together before.

Turning back the clock is tricky. Depending on what's happened, you two may **no longer trust** each other the way you did before you tried out the different roles. The old friendship may take a long time to put back together—if it gets put back together at all.

So think carefully before making the change. If it feels right (only you two can tell), go ahead, but talk it over first. **Promise** you'll treat each other respectfully no matter what. And then be sure you do.

secrets

I like someone at my school. If I tell my best friend, she'll tell the whole school. Then everyone will tease me and laugh at me.

Thea

Talking is a big part of friendship. You and your friends talk constantly about daily stuff—making plans and sharing information. But you probably also talk about personal things—friends, relationships, and feelings. Telling a friend your **private** thoughts makes you feel closer to her, and feeling close feels good. Half the fun of having a crush can be talking about it with friends. The problem is that your friends may enjoy sharing as much as you do. Feelings that should stay private can end up anything but.

So, say you really want
something kept secret.
Here are **3 options:**

Your best option
Don't tell anyone. The only secrets you
truly control are the ones you keep to
yourself.

Your next-best option
If you're going to burst if you don't talk,
confide in a person who isn't part of
your life at school—your brother, say, or
a friend who lives on the other side of
town, or your cousin in Colombia.

Your third-best option

If you still want to tell a friend so badly that you're willing to take the risk—and it IS a risk—then tell one friend only, and make it a good one. Think about it before you do anything.

Don't pick a girl you're trying to impress.

Don't pick an on-again, off-again friend.

Don't pick a girl who told your last secret. Some people just can't keep their lips zipped. If your best friend is one of them, you'll be better off recognizing that and confiding in someone else. You might also consider telling a friend who has confided a secret to you. If you've kept hers, there's a better chance she'll keep yours.

how to keep a secret

It's extremely tempting to trade in secrets. Here are a few thoughts to help a girl stay true.

A lot of secrets are told on impulse. So make it a rule to **wait** two full minutes (check a clock) between the time it occurs to you to tell and the time you open your mouth.

The fun of telling a secret lasts a moment. The trouble it can cause may last for days, weeks—sometimes forever. Ask yourself, **"Is it worth it?"**

Remember the look on your **friend's face** the last time she found out that you told one of her secrets.

Remind yourself **how you felt** when somebody broke a promise and told a secret of yours.

What **kind of person** do you want to be? The kind you can trust or the kind you can't? **It's your pick.**

stop and think

Messaging is so easy! Apps are so fun! You 🖤 collecting 😊🌸🍃🦋 🍩🍰🍦👍🖤🍌🌵😱🔍🖤🍿🎨🖤🍨😂🦄🌭🍔🖤🍕☀️

True, true. But here's the deal: what happens on a gadget is **not private.** It *feels* private when you're alone in your room, snug in your pj's as you hit send. But in fact that device is the most public place you visit every day.

A flirty text can be forwarded.

So can one expressing your deepest feelings.

I keep thinking about you. 😊

I'm gay. I think I like you.

Do you like me?

FIRST KISS

SPA Night

Posts can be shared.

An embarrassing photo that was supposed to disappear in seconds can live on as a screenshot and get passed around to half the kids in town.

The same is true with videos and live-streaming. There's always a way that what you do on-screen can go public. Worse, there's no taking anything back. Once something's out there in the digital space, it pretty much lives forever. Think about *that*.

This doesn't mean you have to tie a rock to your phone and throw it in a lake. It just means you should reread what you've written before you hit send. Ask yourself:

Am I going to be sorry I said this tomorrow?

Would I say this if I were talking to this person face-to-face?

How would I feel if everybody I know saw this photo?

If it's a sensitive subject, and your emotions are high, walk away from that device for five minutes. Revise what you've written. Then reread it again.

Geena says that you've been backstabbing me with Tyler, saying I'm stuck-up. I know you like Tyler, too. You are the WORST FRIEND EVER.

Geena says that you told Tyler I've been going around saying I'm the best singer in school. Did you really say that? I just said I was happy with my audition. The thought that you'd run me down to Tyler is really upsetting. I hope it isn't true.

You'll want to use the same **stop-and-think** strategy when it comes to interacting with strangers online.

Some of those people may seem like friends. You may talk a lot to someone who plays the same game or uses the same app. You might link up with someone through an activity or organization. That can be fine and fun, with one very big

BUT . . .

You have to remember that when you're talking to someone online, you can never be sure who that person really is. "Charleyhorse" may be a seventh-grader in New York, as he says he is, but he may be a full-grown man in Florida, too. There is simply no way to be sure.

How can you stay safe and still enjoy yourself online? Glad you asked.

Use apps and sites that are **appropriate for kids** your age. Have your parents help set up the accounts and passwords.

Stay anonymous. Never give out your real name to somebody online. Don't share your town, your school, your phone number, or details of what you look like.

Stay alert. If someone new appears in your social media, chatty and unknown, be wary. It's easy to reveal more about who you are than you intend to. And if anybody starts saying things that make you uncomfortable, log off instantly and tell your folks.

And **no selfies,** however tempted you may be. Friends of friends of friends—we're talking complete strangers—can find their way into forums you thought were controlled. Your selfies should go only to friends you know in the real world, and go direct.

I know all that safety stuff. But this one boy is so nice. I feel closer to him than anybody at school. I can tell him anything. He really understands me. He feels the same way about me. It can't hurt to send a picture. I hope I can meet him someday. I'm sure he's OK.

But you *can't* be sure. That's the whole point. There are people out there who are very good at tricking others. You simply cannot take the chance.

In any case, the day you find yourself seriously crushing on someone you've never met is the day to take a break from the online world. Power down the computer. Call a friend. Walk around the block. Put some air in your bike tires and go for a spin. Online friendships are fun, but nothing can replace sharing good times in person.

61

flirting

When you flirt, you're sending a secret (or not-so-secret) message saying, *I like you.* It could be:

a little smile, a little wink	a shoulder bump

a funny message	gentle teasing

Flirting is affectionate and playful. It's exciting and sweet. Both people have fun and walk away feeling happy.

But you may find that certain kids express an interest in you that feels very different.

all in fun?

Is this OK or not? Choose your answers.

1. Jack snaps your bra strap.

OK   **not OK**

2. You dyed your hair purple. "That's so gay," says Maria.

OK   **not OK**

3. You wear your penguin slippers in a skit. After that, Riley starts calling you Penguin Feet. It makes you giggle.

OK   **not OK**

4. Jason presses himself into you as everybody crowds onto the bus. His friends laugh.

OK   **not OK**

5. You tell Juan, "Those jeans make your butt look good." He looks really embarrassed.

OK   **not OK**

6. Gavin tells you, "Those jeans make your butt look good." You're really embarrassed.

OK   **not OK**

7. Kyle sends you a message with a photograph of a half-dressed woman that creeps you out.

OK   **not OK**

8. You and Khir are texting. He says, "I like that fish on your shirt. Is it a snook?"

OK   **not OK**

9. Theo looks at you as if you're his favorite dessert. You don't like it. And he seems to know that.

OK   **not OK**

10. You've told Sam three times that you don't want to be his girlfriend. Today he says, "When do I get my kiss?"

OK   **not OK**

Answers

OK

3 is flirting, and **8** is a compliment from a guy who's interested in fish.

Not OK

Everywhere else, one kid is making another kid uncomfortable by:

★ making comments about people's bodies

★ making other kinds of sexually charged comments

★ unwanted touching or ogling

★ using "gay" as an insult

★ sending sexual photos and using dirty language

Why do kids do this? They might think they're flirting. Or they might like showing off and not know when to stop. Boys in particular often want to be daring. A boy might push the edges of what's considered private and polite and be clueless about how it affects other people. But he might also be a bully who knows exactly what he's doing. Upsetting and intimidating people may be his goal.

Whatever the deal is, a girl's best response is to shut this behavior down hard. Any kid worth your time—and your friendship—will stop.

bullying & harassment

Every day at school, boys make fun of me about my body.
I sit off to the side, but they still go on, even though they
know it hurts and embarrasses me.

Megan

Of course, if you've got a bully on your hands, he or she may not stop.

Bullies might make fun of a girl's weight or her looks or the size of her
breasts. A bully might troll a kid online, writing cruel things where the
world can read them—day after day after day. Bullies might send a girl
gross messages or photos, using nasty language. They might grab a girl
in a sexual way without her permission and threaten worse. Bullies can
be especially horrid to kids whose sexuality or way of expressing themselves doesn't fit what the bullies think of as "normal."

There's a term for this: **sexual harassment.** It's cruel. It's also against
the law.

65

When you're sexually harassed, hiding in your locker may seem more logical than trying to stop the bullies. But bullies *can* be stopped if you get help. They want you scared and isolated. So what you need to do is speak up.

You can start by talking to your **parents.** They can't fix this themselves, but they can advocate for you in the adult world in ways you can't.

For instance, they can help you make a **record** of everything the bullies have done. The key is to be specific. Write down the days and places things happened, along with the names of anybody who was there. Make a record of bad phone calls. Make copies of posts, messages, and voicemails.

POSTS THE KIDS HAVE MADE

WHAT'S HAPPENED

Tuesday, May 5
Trevor and Owen waited for me after school and followed me home, calling me names and talking about my body. Rachel was with me part of the time.

Wednesday, May 6
In first period, Julie said that Trevor had started a page called "Is Zoe the Ugliest Girl Alive?" People are posting on it.

Trevor, Owen, and Julius came up to me at lunch and asked if I'd seen their new web page. Owen tried to show it to me. I was with Rachel, Gabby, and Aaliyah.

Thursday, May 7
I had three mean texts on my phone from Jada.

You and your parents can then talk to the **adults at school**—your teacher, a counselor, the principal, and the school's Title IX coordinator. (A Title IX coordinator is a person with special responsibilities in the fight against sexual harassment.) Give them the records you've made and ask them to create a plan to shut the bullies down. That plan might include taking away privileges these kids now enjoy, like riding the bus. It could include suspensions. It should definitely include talking to the bullies' parents.

To make sure all this happens, your parents can put the complaint **in writing** to the school system. Use the words "bullying," "sexual harassment," and "discrimination." The people who run your school have a responsibility to make it a safe place where all kids can go and learn. Your family has every right to expect them to do so.

If you're harassed online, you should report that, too. Social-media sites can remove posts and ban bullies for violating their guidelines. Internet and cell-phone providers can also revoke accounts. Again, your parents can help you collect the evidence you'll need to show what's happened.

In the most extreme cases, you can also go to the **police.** Their job is to enforce the laws, including ones designed to prevent situations like this.

You may be reading this thinking:

Those thoughts are completely understandable. But they are also the thoughts the bullies want you to have. They *want* your silence. They're depending on it. It's what lets them walk around the halls full of themselves while you're afraid to go to school.

So tell. Get help.
Find your allies.

It's the first step to getting your life back. Take that shame you feel and put it where it belongs—on the bullies.

jealousy

It's not uncommon for friends to like the same person. That can mean trouble.

Flirty friend

I have a big crush on this guy in my class. My best friend knows that I like him. Then one time I was spending the night at her house, and she told me she had a crush on him, too. Now they sit next to each other in class, and she flirts with him.

Left Out

If you and this boy were a pair, your friend shouldn't do anything to break things up. But having a crush on the guy doesn't make him yours. There isn't really anything wrong with her talking to him in class. Joke with your friend about how jealous you are and hope for a new seating chart.

The wrong crush

My best friend has had a boyfriend for a year now, and I have a crush on him. I can't tell her or him or anybody!
Sarah

Having a crush on a friend's boyfriend comes pretty naturally. He might be the first boy you've talked to and spent time with. There isn't always a clear line between enjoying a boy's company and feeling romantic. But you should remind yourself that this boy is off-limits. Be sure that nothing you do or say implies anything else. Turn your attention elsewhere. Chat up this boy's good buds. Dive into your guitar lessons—turn up the amp, sing some sad songs. Call another friend. Tell yourself this crush is temporary. You're going to keep your eye on what matters most: your friendship.

Two-faced friend

A girl in my class likes the boy I like! She tries to get his attention every day. But when his back is turned— boom! She's my friend.
Jealous

You shouldn't get mad at this girl for being friendly to a boy she likes unless you think she'd be right to be mad at you for the same thing. But if she's ignoring you one minute and goes super friendly the next, that's not so great. Competing for the same person should never mean turning your back on a friend.

Jealous[10]

I really like this boy in my class. One day at recess, some of the girls (well, about ten) were talking about which boy they liked. ALL of them said the boy I like!!! Now I keep telling myself how bad the other girls are when deep inside I know they're not bad at all!
Miserable in Michigan

You know what's eating you, and that's going to make this situation a whole lot easier to take. It's as you say: These girls aren't bad. They're just like you. And how weird would it be to blame them for that? Your best bet is to be friendly to everybody and see what happens. And don't forget to have some laughs with your friends about how many of you there are. Ten girls! A hockey team—plus subs!

Guilty feelings

I have loved a boy for over one year, but he's going out with one of my best friends. I heard that he was going to break up with her. I was happy at first, but then I thought about how sad my friend would be. But I'm still happy about it. Is that real, real bad?
Happy but Sad

It's not real, real bad, because you feel guilty about it. It shows you care about your friend and don't want to betray her. Act on that, and you'll be OK. If the breakup happens, put her first. Listen to her talk. Give her time to get over him. At that point, you can begin to tell her how you feel. Once you two talk it through, you can look at this boy with a clear conscience.

dances & parties

Gak! It's your first dance. So many questions!

Q. I like the idea of a dance, but I know I'll feel nervous. I'm not dating anybody. Should I just stay home?

A. No way. Go! There must be plenty of other kids who aren't part of a couple. Make plans to go with some of them. It's always nice to have someone to walk in with. You can hang out together by the cheese doodles while you're getting the feel of the room. When you get your courage up, you can start dancing in a pack.

Q. What do I wear?

A. Call your friends and find out what they're wearing. Then open your closet and pick something that makes you feel good.

Q. This dance is at someone's house. My parents won't let me go. What do I do?

A. You could ask your parents to talk to the adults in charge of the party. If your parents knew more about what's planned for the event and what sort of supervision there will be, they might change their minds. Otherwise, you need to respect their decision.

Q. I don't know how to dance. What if somebody asks me?

A. Say, "I'm new at this, but here goes." Then get up and give it a try. Start moving around. Check out what other kids are doing. Borrow a move from the kid to your left. See how that works with the music. Borrow a move from someone else. See what feels right. You may not be the smoothest dancer out there, but, hey, you're learning. The more you keep at it, the more relaxed you'll be. And when the next song starts, you'll already be a little closer to making those moves your own.

Q. That was fun! Now I'd kind of like to have a party at my own home where kids can dance.

A. Talk to your parents. If it's OK with them, they'll set a time and some rules and help you decide how to set everything up. Invite your real friends—not people you think would look good at a party. You'll want some snacks, but they don't have to be fancy. (Who doesn't like popcorn, right?) Ask your friends for their favorite dance songs, so you can make a playlist. And make sure there's something for people to do besides dance. If you have a table game—pool, table tennis, air hockey—you're home free. You could also set out board games or cards, or have a movie going at one end of the room.

friends vs. crush

A girl may find herself torn between her friends and a crush.

Defending your choice

I really like this guy, but my friends think he's a nerd. I can't lie and say that now I think he's a nerd. They already know I like him.

Boy Troubled

It's not easy to stand up to friends who belittle the boy you like. You may worry about their friendship and doubt your own judgment. It might seem safer to put your heart in the fridge—to like the boys your friends like and dismiss the boys your friends dismiss. But what does that get you? Friends you can't be honest with. Boys you don't much like. The feeling of defeat that comes with throwing away your own convictions.

So what's the best thing to do if your friends say this boy's a joke? Tell them why they're wrong.

Him vs. her

My boyfriend and my best friend hate each other. Every day it's "Why are you her friend?" from my boyfriend and "Why don't you break up with him?" from my best friend. I'm always trapped. They are nasty to each other, and I'm sick of it.

Caught in the Middle

Yeesh. What an unpleasant situation. Both your friend and your boyfriend are out of line. Tell them so. To this boy, say: "I know you don't like my friend, but I do. Please stop nagging me about her." Say the same thing to your friend. You can't ask these two to be friends, but you can ask them to stop bugging you. Demand a truce.

Bad guy

My friend has a boyfriend who's no good. He is mean to little kids, and he wrote her a bad note about her old boyfriend. My friend doesn't realize all he's doing, and if I tell her, she might be mad at me.

Texas Girl

If there are things this boy's done that your friend doesn't know about, you can tell her. Just be sure to be specific. "He's not nice" is open to debate. "Last Friday, he made Cece Brook's little brother give him his hat" provides actual information. Tell her what you know and then stop. Don't keep referring to it. Your friend will have to decide for herself whether she wants this boy around. Your role as a friend is to support her.

Fear of friends

A boy I like just asked me out, and I said yes. Now I'm afraid my friends won't like me or will think I'm a loser because they don't like him. Should I break up or lose my friends?
Puzzled in Providence

Whoa. Sometimes a girl looks at a kid with her own eyes and sees romance. Then she looks at her crush through her friends' eyes and has second thoughts. But you're worried about your friends' opinion before they've even had a chance to offer it. You're worried too much, too soon.

The question isn't should you break up or lose your friends. The question is why you doubt your own judgment. You like this boy. Why wouldn't they? And would they really drop you as a friend if they didn't?

Give your friends some credit, and the boy a chance. Tell your friends that you've accepted the invite and why you like the guy. See where it all goes. Could be fun!

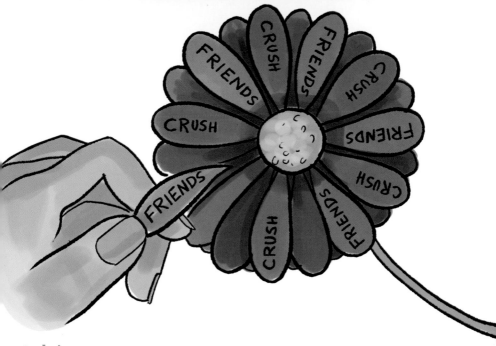

Judging a guy

I like this guy. The problem is, all my friends say I shouldn't. They think he is mean and inconsiderate, but he's always been extremely kind to me.
To Trust Friends (or Not!)

He's kind to you—so far, so good. But if your friends say he's mean, give him a closer look. Watch how he treats other people. What's he like with your friends? With the popular kids? With the unpopular kids? What's he like with adults and younger kids? When two people first like each other, both are on their best behavior. But best behavior isn't regular behavior. And it's this boy's regular behavior that's going to tell you who he really is. It takes time to get to know someone, which is one big reason to go slow with any crush.

Trouble with his buds

There's this boy in my class, and we started going out. He really liked me, but one day he broke up with me because one of his friends doesn't like me. It really hurt because he broke up with me by telling me how much he hates me.
Marty

You've learned the hard way what to expect from people who let their friends do their thinking for them. This guy's made you a sadder, wiser girl—but the sadness won't last. The wisdom will.

peer pressure

Who's running your life? Circle your answer.

1. You tell your friends you've got a crush on a certain girl. They say, "What? That weirdo?" You say,
  a. "She's cool. I like her."
  b. "You think so? How come?"
  c. "Just joking. That girl is such a loser."

2. Your friend says, "Jamil likes you. I'll go tell him you like him back. Then you two will be going together." You feel as if someone stepped on your stomach. You say,
  a. "No, thanks. I don't want to go with anybody. And if I did, I'd arrange it myself."
  b. "But, but, but—I don't know about this."
  c. "OK."

3. Maureen is the most popular girl in school. She appears at your locker one day and says, "Why do you spend so much time with Hal? I could fix you up with Eddie." You say,
  a. "I like Hal."
  b. "I wouldn't want you to go to all that trouble."
  c. "Ur, great, I guess."

4. You and your buddy George are having a great time, as always, when Kristi and her gang appear. She says, "Now we know who your boyfriend is!" You say,
a. "Whatever, Kristi."
b. "No, no, it's not what you think. We're just friends. Really!"
c. Nothing. You're blushing from head to toe. And you'll say nothing to George from now on, either.

5. Four boys showed up at the party, and here you are playing Truth or Dare. Jillian demands that you go in the back room with Will and kiss. Will's willing. You're not. You say,
a. "No. I don't take that kind of dare."
b. "I have a cold."
c. "Oh, all right."

Answers

In charge

If you answered mostly **a's,** you sail your own ship. You love your friends, but you don't let them tell you what to do. If you get involved with a kid, it's going to be because you want to—not because somebody else thinks you should.

Wishy-washy

If you answered mostly **b's,** you know what you want but are too cowed by your friends to say so. Try being up-front. You may be surprised at how well it works— and pleased with how you feel about yourself afterward.

Bossed around

If you answered mostly **c's,** your friends are pulling your strings. You've got your own brain and your own beliefs. It's time to act on them! You're going to find yourself in one ratty situation after the next until the day you say, "No, I'm deciding this myself."

why pair off?

What's a good reason to make it official? Circle your answers.

1. Your best friend says you should.

2. Your crush is nice, brainy, cute, and fun to be with.

3. Also SUPER popular.

4. All your other friends have paired up, and you don't want to be left out.

5. All the popular kids are dating.

6. You want to make someone else jealous.

7. You can't say no to "Do you want to be my girlfriend?"

8. You've got a crush on this kid's best friend.

9. You feel good when you're around this person.

10. This is the only person who's asked, and you want to go with SOMEbody.

11. You don't want your friends to think you're too scared.

12. It's what girls your age do.

Answers

Good reasons: 2 and 9. **Bad reasons:** All the rest.

Explanation: Do you really need one?

things to do together

Many kids date without ever going anywhere together at all. But that doesn't have to be the case. There are lots of things kids can do as couples to have fun. For starters:

Your dog needs a bath. One of you can suds her up, while the other handles the hose. Watch out, world!

How about a round of **mini golf?** Show no mercy.

Summertime? Lovely. You two and your friends can all meet at the **pool.**

How about **bowling?** Bumpers? Don't even think about it.

So your brother's on the basketball team at the high school? Cool. Invite your special person to **go to a game** with your family.

Sigh. Time for **chores.** But, hey, what if you do them together?

Sledding. It's not just for first-graders. Maybe Mom can make hot cocoa afterward.

Hungry? Stop at the bagel shop. See what weird stuff they're putting in the cream cheese today.

OK, there's always **shopping.** Just make sure you stop in places that you both have an interest in.

It's open gym. Don't just stand there. Get a volleyball game together. Dodgeball works, too.

You wanted to see that **movie,** right? The two of you can get a little group together. Your dad can drive.

Sit on the steps and talk.

Having tickets to a water park is great, but just hanging out with someone you like can be even better. It's the **spirit** you bring to what you do that matters.

touching

When you were a baby, you enjoyed getting cuddled and stroked. When you got a little older, you enjoyed sitting on your parents' laps and feeling their arms around you. Even now, you may like having a friend comb your hair and braid it, and like the feeling you get walking down the street with your arm flung over a friend's shoulders. There's something wonderful about touching a person you care for. There may come a time when you will enjoy a physical relationship in a romance, too.

Romantic touching usually begins with holding hands, a first dance, or a first kiss. That first kiss can be wonderful and magical. It can be awkward and disappointing. It can be goofy and sweet. Whatever the experience, lots of older people can still remember everything about it.

I was in first grade, delivering a May basket. This boy popped out of the house and told me the tradition was that if you gave somebody a May basket, he got to kiss you. I didn't know any better, so I let him do it. I didn't have another kiss till I was a senior in high school.
Susie

I was 12. I'd been going out with my twin brother's best friend since fourth grade, but we hadn't gone anywhere, let alone kissed. My brother thought this was awful. One day when the three of us were playing football, he said the loser had to kiss the winner. Then he made sure I lost. So I kissed Mark (it was quick!), and we continued to play. My brother was so proud of himself.
Jeannine

I was in fourth grade. We'd just learned the rules for spin the bottle. The first time I kissed Jane, I hardly knew what to do. She turned her head so I barely grazed her cheek, and in the process I sneezed. The best was when Jane kissed me. Her lips scarcely touched the corner of my mouth, but her hair brushed my face, I smelled her sweetness, and her eyes closed.
Tom

I was 14. The boy I had a crush on took me to his mother's wedding. After the ceremony, we took a walk, and he kissed me behind a tree. I floated all the way home.
Harriet

My first kiss was a first miss. Kent asked, "Well, can I?"
I said, "I guess so." He put the arm that wasn't carrying
the football around my waist. I closed my eyes and felt his
forehead graze my ear. Then came a sort of muffled snort.
He seemed to be smelling my hair. "Well, I guess, bye," he
muttered, and then sprinted away. There was clearly something unkissable about me. I wept. An entire miserable week
later, Kent confessed that he had truly intended to kiss me
but had, in fact, missed.
Judy

I was 14. I was watching a movie outdoors at the day camp
where I worked, and I was kissed by this boy I'd had a crush
on for months. I was so euphoric I didn't eat for three days,
and my mom took me to the doctor.
Deb

The summer before seventh grade, my cousin double-dog-
dared me to kiss Aaron behind the pool. She thought that
because we shared the same first name, we were destined to
be together. She was wrong. The kiss lasted two seconds—
one second longer than the relationship. My cousin was
promptly fired from matchmaking duties.
Erin

it's up to you

To kiss or not to kiss? If you're leaning "yes," be sure this is a person you know well and trust. Keep it private. And be sure you actually want to do what you're doing. There's no need to rush into kissing. It is not a competition. Just because your friend kissed a kid last week doesn't mean you have to run out and kiss someone tomorrow. And you shouldn't kiss somebody because they pressure you into it, either. That goes for all other touching, too. If someone gets pushy, push back. If you hear:

Please! You're hurting my feelings. You must not like me if you don't. You did it before, so you owe it to me. I'm going to drop you if you don't. You're so mean. What's the big deal? All the other girls would do it. If you did it with anybody else, you should do it with me. Please?

LAY IT ON THE LINE.

No. I'm not going to do anything I don't want to do. If you've got a problem with that, then I've got a problem with you.

trouble starters

There are a hundred tried-and-true ways to stir up trouble in a relationship. What are the things that bug people the most?

If someone talks non-stop about nothing.
Ian, age 12

They worry about their hair and clothes and what they look like.
Molly, age 12

Being all perky is annoying. So is never giving an honest point of view.
Connor, age 12

When girls pressure you to do everything. You're supposed to be the one who calls them. They get mad if you don't.
Joey, age 13

When girls text too much. If they have to text, they should do it once and get the whole story, not five times.
Andrew, age 13

If a boy flirts with other girls and talks about other girls to you.
Meredith, age 13

If someone talks about themselves too much and acts full of themselves.
Jessie, age 13

When a girl talks a lot, takes a long time in stores, complains, and does the "like-like-like" thing.
Aaron, age 13

When boys aren't themselves. They try to be cool and wind up acting really stupid.
Jenny, age 13

When they ignore you if they're with their friends.
Luba, age 13

Some boys pressure girls to do things they don't want to do.
Laura, age 13

When someone doesn't talk to you and almost avoids you.
Megan, age 12

When a girl acts all depressed, like "Oh, you hate me," for no reason.
Ike, age 13

solving problems

You're mad. Or your sweetheart's mad. Or you're both mad. Does that mean it's over? Not necessarily.

What's the problem? Think before you blow up. Decide what's bugging you. Is it really what happened this morning or is it something entirely different, which you've been brooding about all week? Think about it. Talk it over with your big sister or your mom or dad. Get it clear in your head. You can't fix a problem until you know for sure what it is.

Pick a good time. Some conversations are doomed because of when and where they take place. It's just not a good idea to launch into a topic that upsets both of you 30 seconds before the bell rings. You need privacy. You need time.

Express yourself. Explain what you're unhappy about and what you want to have happen.

Listen. Be ready to listen to the other side, too. If your sweetheart seems reluctant to talk and impatient to get the conversation over with, say, "I know this is hard to talk about, but I think it's important that we figure this out."

Don't be afraid to disagree. You know how to compromise and negotiate, and that's great. But it's just as important to say what you think. So find your courage and be honest. And don't get offended by a person who does the same thing. Some people express themselves more bluntly when they disagree.

Expect some outbursts. Chances are, you'll both get excited and say some things you don't mean. When you hear yourself going over-board, admit it: "I'm exaggerating, but that's how it felt!"

Make a plan. Try to walk away with some kind of plan to make things better. "OK. I'll go now, and let's talk after dinner." Even if you're both still riled up inside, it's going to feel good to have agreed on something.

problem partners

You don't want to let a problem partner walk all over you. You also don't want to throw a nice one away over a misunderstanding.

Broken promises

I have a boyfriend who keeps promising to do things but then doesn't. But he also does nice things for me. Should I dump him or not?
Unsure

How firm are the promises? If he says, "I'll meet you at four," and then offers no apology when he forgets, that's bad. But it could also be that he's saying things to be nice but doesn't really think of them as commitments. Where you hear "I will," he thinks he's saying "I could." If he's being nice in other ways, maybe you can live with it. You can also express how you feel: "You said you were going to help me rake the yard. Then you didn't. I was annoyed." See how he responds and judge from that.

Phone shy

My boyfriend never calls me, so I have to call him. One time, I called him and asked him why, and he said, "I'm busy, and I'm never free to talk." All I said was, "Well, try, at least." And he said he had to go. What does this mean? Should I dump him?
Hannah

Not necessarily. Your boyfriend doesn't like to talk on the phone—that much is clear. A lot of boys don't. Talking is often a big part of girls' friendships. Put two girls in a room, and they may well sit on the rug and chat. Put two boys in a room, and they're more likely to start throwing a ball or lock on to a video game. There are always exceptions, but in general intimate conversations aren't as central in boys' relationships. So you'd be wise not to expect the same kind of back-and-forth of texts and calls with a boyfriend that you get with a friend.

What's your relationship like with this boy otherwise? Do you have fun when you see each other at school? Does he seem to enjoy your company when you're together other times? If so, don't make a big issue over the phone.

Neglectful

I think my boyfriend doesn't like me very much. He pays more attention to other girls than to me.

Amber

First, a quick double-check: Ask yourself if you're sure about this. Dating doesn't mean that you two stop talking to the rest of the world. Both of you deserve to talk to friends and classmates freely, just like you did before you started dating.

If you *are* sure—if he flirts with other girls and ignores you—then you should talk to him about it. If you don't hear something like "I'm sorry. I still like you best," you need to pull the plug on this guy. You deserve to be treated well. Don't settle for anything less.

are you the problem?

What's the smart move for a girl who cares about a relationship?
Circle your answers.

1. You're coming out of class when you see your boyfriend talking to three girls. You march up and say, "Why are you flirting with them?"

good move   **bad move**

2. You're supposed to be a couple, right? You say, "What are you doing this afternoon? What are you doing tonight? What are you doing tomorrow? What are you doing this weekend?"

good move   **bad move**

3. You're talking to the most popular boy in the school. Your boyfriend walks by. You ignore him.

good move   **bad move**

4. You two were planning to meet at the store, but now a text pings in: "Sorry! I forgot I have soccer practice." You respond, "No problem," and go do something else.

good move   **bad move**

5. You and your friends are talking nonstop. Your boyfriend is quiet. You could try bringing him into the conversastion, but you don't. He's not really one of you.

good move   **bad move**

6. Your girlfriend really ticked you off this morning. To punish her, you threaten to dump her.

good move   **bad move**

Answers

1. Bad move.

Unless this boy lives in a cave 50 miles from town, he's going to have friendships with other people. Get used to it. If you can't, your jealousy is going to make life miserable for you both.

2. Bad move.

Make a kid report to you all the time about where she goes and who she sees, and she'll feel like a dog on a two-inch leash. First chance she gets, she'll bolt. And who can blame her?

3. Bad move.

Come on! How two-faced is that? This isn't some game where you toss a person onto the discard pile the minute you see a chance to pick up a higher card.

4. Good move.

Being relaxed is always a good move. Don't take everything personally.

5. Bad move.

Consider how you'd feel if the person you're dating ignored you in front of his or her friends. Awkward, left out, hurt. Maybe resentful. Including everybody in the conversation is basic kindness.

6. Bad move.

If you've got a problem, deal with it. Making threats is fighting dirty.

time to break up?

There are times a girl should walk away from a relationship and times she shouldn't. What would you do in these situations?

1. You go to the movies with your boyfriend. He sees his friends, leaves you, and sits with them. Stuff like this has been going on for weeks.

hold on   **break up**

2. This is the only person you've ever liked, but being together has been *so* frustrating this week.

hold on   **break up**

3. You decided to go with this kid because you were curious to see what it would be like. Now you know. It's weird and awkward and complicated, and you wish you were free to be yourself again.

hold on   **break up**

4. Your girlfriend is nice and all, but the truth is you've started liking somebody else. You don't want to hurt her feelings.

hold on   **break up**

5. You can't get your boyfriend on the phone. Is he ghosting you?

hold on   **break up**

Answers

The best answer to 2 and 5 is hold on. If you're frustrated or worried about something, talk it over. Don't throw out a good relationship before you try to fix things.

The best answer to 1, 3, and 4 is break up.

There's no reason to stay with a person who treats you badly. Now or ever. And there's no point in staying with someone if your heart isn't in it either.

Ending a relationship isn't easy. But it's a whole lot easier than getting up every day knowing that you're in a relationship that isn't right.

how to break up

You know **it's got to be done.** But if you're like most girls, you're feeling a little chicken.

Could you go to Antarctica and call from there? Or what if you pretended you had amnesia? Maybe if your friends all said you died . . . Oh, wait! You could just ghost the person by ignoring them! They'll get the idea eventually; and in the meantime, you can pretend like nothing's happening, and nobody's getting hurt.

Nice try, but no. Ghosting may be easier than moving to Antarctica, but it's no better as an option. A lot of nice girls do cruel things at moments like this because they feel awkward about delivering bad news. Don't be one of them. You've got to do it right and have the talk **face-to-face.**

Talking at school may be convenient, but there are too many people around. Find a different place. Keep the conversation **private.**

Put some thought into what you'll say beforehand. It should be more than "I don't want to date you anymore." Give an honest **reason.** But don't be mean.

"I liked it better when we were just friends"

"I appreciate all the fun we've had, but I want to see other people"

"We don't get along that well"

is better than

"I'm sorry I ever said I'd go out with you."

"You really bug me."

"You're a jerk."

Will any of these lines produce a smile and, "That's OK"? Not likely. This person will still be hurt and might be angry—but not nearly so hurt and angry as if you ended things in a way that showed you were thinking only of yourself. And after a day or two, your old crush may be as relieved as you are to be out of the relationship.

getting dumped

A few weeks ago, my boyfriend and I broke up. The reason I am taking it so hard is that I really thought he was "The One."

Lonely in Texas

Dumped. What a word. Garbage gets dumped. And garbage is a pretty accurate description of what it feels like when someone dumps you.

Sometimes you can see trouble coming. You know things aren't right. But before you do something about it, *wham.* You've been dumped. A blow to the pride? Sure. Yet when the dust settles, you may find your feelings are fine.

Of course, there are also times when the dump comes as a total surprise from someone you still really like. What do you do then? The same kinds of things you've always done when bad things happen.

Talk to your mom or dad, your sister or brother, your bestie Keisha or your Aunt Maeve. Pick a good shoulder to cry on, and let it out.

When you're out of tears, go for a run. Break out the skateboard or the bike or the tennis racket. Make a point to do something physical every day.

Call friends. **Make plans.** Stay connected. Keep things moving. Don't sit around feeling sorry for yourself.

You may have things that remind you of this person—letters, pictures, the T. rex eraser with purple hearts. Remind yourself that no good can come from brooding over these relics. Give them one last sigh and then pitch them.

Face forward, not back. Put your mind to taking care of you.

taking care of you

how are you doing?

Have crushes changed the way you think?

1. Ever since school started, you've felt bad because no one has any interest in you. You haven't dated once. You've started making lists in your head of all the things that are wrong with you.

That's me.   **That's not me.**

2. Darla told Dan that you liked Dennis, and Dan told Doug. Doug likes you, so he got discouraged and told Deb. Deb likes Dennis, so she got mad and told lies about you and Dan to Diane, who repeated them at the dance to Dennis, who told Darla he didn't like you anymore. Darla told you in the doughnut shop. You got mad and wrote a note to Dennis. You had Denise give it to Dane to give to Dennis, only Dane had a dentist appointment and left early. So you called Dennis that night. Then you called Darla and Deb and Dan and Doug and Denise and Dane. Turns out that Denise was mad at Deb . . .

Then you walk into Spanish and realize—*today's the test!*

That's me.   **That's not me.**

3. You are crazy, crazy about one particular kid. If you had to choose between this crush and your best friend, you'd go with the crush.

That's me.   **That's not me.**

4. No one will ever like you. You're too ugly. Pretty girls fill you with feelings you don't even want to discuss.

That's me.   **That's not me.**

5. Kiernan wants you to come to the park after dark. "So what if your parents say you can't. Don't be a wuss." You go. You'd do anything for Kiernan.

That's me.   **That's not me.**

Answers

If you said **that's me,** here's what you need to know:

1. Having lots of dates doesn't make you a better person. Having none doesn't make you a worse one. Judge yourself on character, not conquests.

2. Trying to talk to an entire school is like fighting a monster with seven heads. Keep it simple. If you have a problem with a person, go to that person. Don't use messengers. Don't be one.

3. Look around. How many couples do you see that have lasted more than a month? More than a year? The fact is, crushes come and go in a girl's life. Good friends don't. Friendships are precious. Don't throw one away over a crush.

4. You're not ugly! Girls have always struggled with the idea of beauty, but these days most girls grow up comparing themselves to models and celebrities. It's hard not to. Pretty people are everywhere, from the phone in your pocket to the windows of stores. Small wonder if a girl thinks, *I'll never look like that. It's hopeless.*

It's not. No matter what you look like. Yes, beauty counts in romance. And, yes, some girls will always be considered prettier than others. But beauty is far more varied than those ultra-skinny, ultra-perfect people you see on-screen. You'll find it in the faces of all your friends. Look now, and see if that isn't true. Too, there's an endless list of things that make a person attractive that have nothing to do with looks at all—things like character, creativity, conviction, and heart. And every single one matters more than the shape of your nose or a number on a scale. Rely on that.

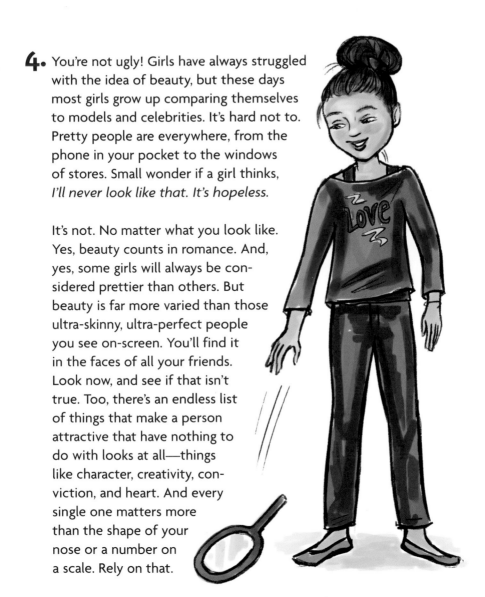

And know this: you'll find someone who loves you. That person might not show up this year or the year after that. But she or he is out there. And that person will be in love with *you*, not with your face.

5. Don't get stupid. A girl who'll do anything to please a crush wins nobody's respect. Not that person's. Not her own. Do what you know is right and stand up for what you deserve.

happy ever after

You've had ups and downs with friends over the years. You're going to have ups and downs with romance, too. It's all part of **growing up.**

What you want to remember along the way is this: You've got so much to find out about yourself—interests to explore, talents to develop. Sure, relationships will be important to you. But your happiness doesn't depend on hitching yourself to the partner of your dreams. It depends on finding out what you love to do in the world and doing it. Put your faith in you—in your hopes for the future, your plans for what you can do and create, experience and enjoy. It'll make you strong and confident and ready for anything, including **love.**

All comments and suggestions received by American Girl
may be used without compensation or acknowledgment.
Sorry—photos can't be returned.

Here are some other American Girl books you might like:

Each sold separately. Find more books online at americangirl.com.

Parents, request a FREE catalog at **americangirl.com/catalog.**
Sign up at **americangirl.com/email** to receive the latest news and exclusive offers.

Discover online games, quizzes, activities,
and more at **americangirl.com/play**